WHO SAYS YOU CAN'T PLAY SONGS ABOUT DEATH ON HOSPITAL RADIO?

a poetry collection by
C A I T L I N T H O R N L E Y

Copyright © 2020 Caitlin Thornley.

All rights reserved. This book or any portion thereof may not be reproduced or used in any manner whatsoever without the express written permission of the author except for the use of brief quotations embodied in critical reviews and certain other non-commercial uses permitted by copyright law.

ISBN: 9781652946571

First printing edition 2020.

Author photo by Tegan Thornley.
Cover and illustrations by Caitlin Thornley.

For the Thornleys, the Sawyers and everyone in between.

CONTENTS

A good start	…1
House of straw	…2
Confidence (?)	…4
Sixteen-year-old politics	…5
Roadtrip	…9
Unnamed	…10
I like you	…11
"Yes, I know what you mean."	…12
Black hole	…13
Honey	…17
The technicalities of an argument	…18
Just like coffee	…23
WRATH	…25
We are	…29
Togetherness	…30
Sheep(s)	…31
Universal	…32
Swim	…34
restart me	…35
The Good Man	…39

CONTENTS

Unnamed 2	…40
To never be looked at	…41
Like the stars	…42
World changer	…43
When you talk	…47
I don't think I fit in in Heaven (I'll try Hell)	…48
Sunset	…49
A teddy bear doesn't breathe	…53
Clouds	…54
Is she a ghost now?	…55
Beach boy	…56
About the weather	…57
Hurting, still	…61
Struggling through silence	…65
You've lost your mind	…66
Stronger than you think	…67
Beginning / end	…71
Wokingham, Berkshire	…72
Grandparents	…75
I grow old	…76

These words were written
to be spoken aloud.

YOU ARE
HERE

A good start

I was born
early,
quickly and
without warning.
A frenzy of kicking and screaming solidified
my objection to containment.

I will continue as I started:
kicking
and
screaming
and

refusing to be contained.

House of straw

I live in a house of straw. I

cower under my straw-stuffed bed
with my straw-stuffed toy
cradled beneath my straw-stuffed head. I

live in fear
of the creature that

skulks past my straw-ridden walls;
he treads my straw-ridden pathways
and straw-tiled halls.

He growls
threatening murmurs that
tempt foreign tears.
I hear foul screams not meant for my ears. I

live in a house of straw.

I am made of easily manipulated materials.
My bones creak
under the weight of
tiptoed funerals
and bold secrets crack my

foundations. I
live in a house of straw.

Worms of tension
riddle my intestines as his
grumbling snarls grow clearer.

My stomach turns to water as the
deafening echo of his cough steps nearer.

I live in a house of straw.

Straw-soaked dread saturates my
straw-stained chest;
I inhale straw-stale air and
try my straw-damned best.

He arrives
wearing a fleece and a frown
and,
with just a single breath,

my

                              walls

            come

                                            tumbling

                          down.

Confidence (?)

Confidence tastes like (?)
a full English breakfast. Like
a black hole,
curtains that don't quite keep out the light.

It tastes like
sickness. (?) Like jam,
like learning to ride a bike, like
saying
I'm sorry
for the first time.

I swallow confidence down.

I taste
(?) rice pudding.
I taste my father's favourite record,
my mother's smile.

Confidence hurls
from my stomach and
I let it dribble
down my chin. It

congeals
under my jaw.

It tastes like
contemplating suicide.
Like electrocution. Like
(?)

Sixteen-year-old politics

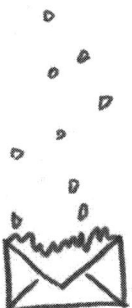

Roadtrip

Amber hazard lights
flash sporadically
and shadow your features haphazardly.
I'm cold, tired and bursting for a wee –
"Go on the side of the road," you suggest,
"But everyone will see!" I protest.

Two minutes later I'm squatting on the side of the M25.
A Ford Fiesta beeps as their headlights flash
over my bare arse.
I give them the two fingers.
Your laugh

lingers

as we drive the rest of the way home.
I'm not alone, I think.

I am not alone.

Unnamed

He has this way of looking at me
that makes me feel like everything I own
is on show.

I like you

I like you like partially squashed homemade sandwiches.
Like Saturday mornings: long and lacking in
responsibility.
Like rain at a family BBQ, like
inevitability,
like going to bed at 9pm.

I like you like the rise and fall of the sun:
constant in our statically changing world.
Like planets pushing and expanding
without known reason
as if they were cosmic playdough.

I like you like Christmas trees in late November.
Like smiling like you mean it.
Like freshly hoovered carpets, like fluffy socks,
like the sound of thunder on Tuesdays:
comfortable.

I like you like walks in the Lake District. Like
waterfalls and stones and
scraped knees with stories. Like adventure
and like wishing
for nothing more.

"Yes, I know what you mean."

I can't stop thinking about that thing you said
that late June afternoon, head
dizzy from pints of
fizzy beer and cider and lager and
doesn't it all taste the same?

We watched the football game.
World Cup, twenty eighteen
(I don't remember what teams).

Stumbling through fields, vision
misted by beer and cider and lager and
you insisted
that we lay in the grass
and watch the sun sweatily slide past
the horizon.

After time, the air turned black
and chill tickled
my spaghetti-strapped back
as we lay in silence.

In that moment,
I suddenly realised that I was alive.
I asked you if you knew what I meant.
You said:
"Yes, I know what you mean."

It would seem
that proper living can come at strange times,

like when you're lying in a field in your hometown,
alcohol (or love) spinning the world as the sun goes down.

Black hole

We sit
in camp chairs that aren't ours.
I'm in my knickers
because, after four vodka Red Bulls,
I pissed on my trousers.
You call me disgusting
but you're smiling
so I don't mind.
Next, we leave the urine-laced chairs
and run around a field
(I've put my trousers back on).
You get given free chicken nuggets
and we share them under a sky
littered with stars
like a teen's untreated acne.
You say you've never felt happier
and suddenly my heart is amongst the planets
and, in the weightless bliss of now,
I hardly hear the collision impending.

Honey

Nausea creeps up my throat as I
cling to the garden wall.
Whispers of words
once meant for me
float from the kitchen window like
sour fog.

Peering through the misted glass,
my crumpled heart breaks some more.
I see lust
pour from his mouth like honey
as he holds her a little too tight
and she is a little too familiar
for my fury to
bubble down.

Over her naked shoulder,
my daggers meet his eyes
and, licking honey from his lips, he says:

"Darling! What a … surprise."

The technicalities of an argument

I silently drip feed you adjectives
until you taste the sweet words
that I always wanted you to say.

You swill them around your mouth,
turn them bitter
and spit them back at me.

I try to force feed you commas and exclamation marks
but, as my fist enters your throat, you gag and
regurgitate question marks and full stops
that stain my carpet.

You block me with a semi colon;
I recoil, hurt, but stay quiet.

I am backhanded with an adverb.
Aggressively, you fire spiteful arrows
into my chest until words begin to
trickle from my lips.

I shoot / crack / blast
the malice from your mind
until it dribbles from your nose
and you beg me to stop with
soft / silky / gentle words
that you should have used from the start.

You were a guessing game,
a half-drawn hangman
swinging
through a sky of crossed out letters
and mispronounced words.

My tongue runs from me –

it cascades onto broken plates
and badly kept promises.

Can you hear me now?

~~CAN YOU~~
~~HEAR ME~~
~~NOW?~~

Just like coffee

You send vibrations through my blood that
create addictive sensations, another hit,
another greedy temptation.

And I drink every last drop ///

slop broken tar down myself in haste,
burning my oesophagus on tasteless taste,
what a waste
to continue consuming ~~someone~~
something
that is bad for you.

And I don't know how to stop.

I drink coffee every morning
(I wake up next to you every morning), a
bottomless black mourning, warning me,

dawning on me,
burning, squirming, *calling me*
screaming:

<u>you</u>

are bad for me!

Just like coffee, I clutch you.
I touch you /// need you too much – too
dependent on you.

I drench you in sugar
to sweeten you up
(I can't drink you alone). Coffee tastes like
home

even when it burns my tongue.

I curl up with coffee on the sofa – I wait
for you and the night grows
dark

and darker and darker.
I become something I'm not.

And, just like coffee,
you are bitter
and turn
cold

after a while.

WRATH

slow motion charging at
a speed close to light
too hot to scream too cold to move
yet I come exploding

I SWEAR IF YOU ever ***LAY ANOTHER FINGER***

I don't just throw a punch
with the expectation of you catching
but force it into you until it swallows down

my black mind translated
to black eye

blind
but not physically

nerve endings bruising as
thoughts jump together with a smash
causing irrational ripples
and actions never taken when
calm

blink

back in the room
too hot to scream too cold to move
wanting to explode
yet morals hold me back
and with a face and heart of stone
I leave

alone.

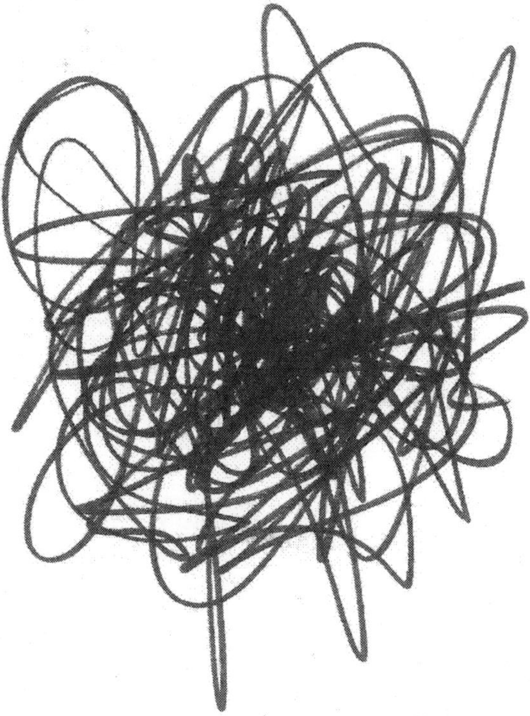

We are

We are
shooting ping pong balls
through messy temporary homes. We
are a gaggle of kids
in their late teens and early twenties
downing liquid courage
to smother our out of date personalities.
We are
scared. We are
less than what we thought we'd be. We
are messily applied eyeliner and
self conscious delusions. We
are charity shop sourced
designer jeans.
We are betting our student loans
on blackjack.
We are charades. We are
promises
scrawled on the back of ripped notebooks.
We are
Morrison's own brand vodka. We
are 39p lemonade and
paper straws.
We are
terrified. We are
more than what we've ever known. We
are inseparable.
We are
way out of our depth. We are
only human.

Togetherness

We sat on your bedroom floor with wine,
doubting how we've lived.

We laughed at things that didn't make sense
and cried at things that did.

- For Katie

Sheep(s)

Sheep crowded in the field
with a force similar to an itch.
I watched them,
as we do,
through barbed wire
and safe distance.

They mewed and I silently responded –
finding myself solemnly agreeing
with their muted sighs
as I stood still,
harbouring the uncomfortable realisation
that I may be
on the wrong side of the fence.

Universal

I feel the planets messily orbit my chest
and the sound of their moons
clattering against one another
slurs into my very speech.

We don't know what's beneath us, really.
Let alone what lies below surfaces of
planets and moons and stars
that are so far
from anything we have ever known.

What is it that lies under layers of skin?
What is beneath eczema and tattoos,
tissue and bone? What are we made of,
really?

I'll volunteer to be snipped open and
cut up into tiny pieces;

scientists will gaggle around my mangled limbs
and rummage between my organs
as they try to find The Answer. I tell them

that I feel universal. Like a planet: isolated.
I am an isolated planet
with a thin crust
and I am ready to break at the lightest of footprints.

No, I am a star
and I am ready to explode. No!
I am a star that exploded
millions of years ago,
yet my cry for help rings lightyears away
from anyone capable of hearing it –
perhaps when my dead, skin-like flakes of stardust

reach you … perhaps then
you will have died too.

And maybe we will return to dust.
Or moons. Or planets, indeed.
Or maybe –
maybe we never left them at all.

Swim

The ocean is a big place:
a room full of emptiness.

Chaotic waves of hello and goodbye and
hello I never thought I'd see you again

methodically beat with my heart.

But the tide turns,
my lungs fill and chaotic waves of goodbye and hello and
goodbye I'll never see you again

systematically unravel instinct
until I am left

suspended

and
wondering what went wrong.

Thinking I was swimming,
but drowning all along.

restart me

restart me //
no backup necessary.
password must contain the middle name
of someone you'd prefer to forget //
restart me.

my keys are jjammed. I can't don't won't
work //
restart me.

forgotten your password?
security question: what colour were his eyes?
    ctrl alt del –

restart me. I show only eRr/;0rs ~   Human
or otherwise.

what is wrong with me?
    ctrl alt del –
    ctrl alt del –

what is wrong with me? please
// restart me.

LOADING

The Good Man

Meaningful hands on my facearmslegschest –
my body now a crime scene. My skin …
a forensic disaster.

You excel in excellence
and your profile fits that of The Good Man.
We believe him.
Like him.   Love him,

perhaps.   ?
But something behind that smile is clueless.
The Good Man
sags.

Veins crawl up your skin:
bright blue, thick and twisting like vines. They
congregate at your neck and
rip him from you.

Corpse-like, they begin questioning.
Bright lights, bold faces, brave queries:
tell me, stranger,
do you even know who you are?

Unnamed 2

I couldn't look at him for long.
I felt as though I might disappear if I did.

To never be looked at

The street light glow highlighted my features*
and I could see your eyes
scanning over my face

*(so far I had succeeded
in hiding behind
the shadow of you)

and I wanted nothing more
than to scale those metal poles
for miles and miles
and smash their burn into darkness.

If I could,
I would climb the evening,
pluck the moon from her podium
and rip her to shreds,

letting the crumbs of nightlight shatter into the air.

I would extinguish the sun, too**:
mimic Icarus – but learn from his mistakes –
and snuff out the glare
with my thumb and forefinger.

**(if only I could!)

Then day would be night
and night would be darker
and you would
never have to see me.

Like the stars

It's seven pm already
and the stars peep round the clouds,
too intimidated by the harsh slap of the lamp post light
to say anything.

I think about you a few times,
letting feelings (like stars) peep into my consciousness
and readily striking them down
when they emit a response from me.

I can't
say anything. Too intimidated by humiliation to say
anything.

The clouds clear and stars blaze in their spots, unmoving.
Several flicker –
scared, still.

Still, they scald the sky.

World changer

"I reckon I'm going to change the world." I say.
We're lying in bed
and have been for the best part of today.
He looks at me, his smile curved in pride and says:
"I don't doubt you will."

I lie still,
my guards up, armed and ready to attack;
prepared for a snigger
or a retort straight back.

But his voice oozes sincerity
like none I've ever heard from a man before.

"I don't doubt you will." he repeats again,
touching his thumb on my chin.

I dismantle my guards and let him in.

When you talk

Bruises crawl from your
mouth like poisonous spiders:
legs tangled in lies.

I don't think I fit in in Heaven (I'll try Hell)

I have been falling for years
and I am unsure why Earth has hesitated to stop me.

Tumbling through atmosphere and atmosphere and – !
I have forgotten which way is up
which way is down which way is left
which way is right?

I stopped screaming in the third week. Learnt to
enjoy the plummeting feeling in my gut.

                Sometimes it feels like flying.

They said it is instinctual. You just

    step
            off

   the

             clouds

   and

             float.

So tell me, why have I been falling like rocks in the sea?

I am ready for this planet to inhale me; I don't think
that I was meant for the sky –

looking down made me feel dizzy and
I never got used to wearing wings.

Sunset

Last night I watched the sun set – it reminded me of you.
Then I watched blackness poison the sky

and that reminded me of you, too.

A teddy bear doesn't breathe

A teddy bear sits
in the arms of a child.
Another duplicate of
twins of twins of twins – nothing special.

His fur smells like something familiar, homely –
like a roast dinner and Ariel washing powder.
Hope pushes hard against the back
of his buttoned eyes and
his embroidered smile attracts Kind Doctor.

Stuffing oozes from his stomach like treacle
and his fur comes off in patches,
leaving him cold, damp and exposed.

He doesn't move as Doctors come in and out, pushing
needles into his deflated chest and
fixing his broken bits with a mere bandage.
The fabric unravels and falls
to the floor.
He doesn't pick it up.

Now he smells like morphine and anti-bacterial wipes.
A lot of his fur is missing
and the stitches have come loose on his smile.

He sits, lopsided, on the bed.
His eyes don't hold hope anymore.
They are just black beads rooted
in a badly sewn mind.

His head droops
like Sympathetic Doctor.
A teddy bear doesn't breathe.

Clouds

Today I watched the clouds as I cried
and wondered how they move so calmly
when they hold great thunderstorms
so deep within.

Is she a ghost now?

She is not invisible –
you cannot see invisible. I see
her
like you see the breeze
as it changes everything you can feel
without stopping to even think
of asking for permission.

In the storm, she is the scintillation.
In the tsunami she sisters the crash – always gone
before you can catch her
(and they have tried to catch her)!

I want to keep her
but you cannot cage a hurricane
for it will certainly ravage itself into a
nightmare.

        Once
she sat for a while. Still.
Her chaos
muted.

I forced the world to stop
and held my breath, watching.

                Terrified
that if someone were to sigh too forcefully,
she would simply disintegrate
and crumble away.

Beach boy

Your mouth: a beach, stretching
for miles. Welcoming on a good day. On a bad day …
stormy and wild.

It has been years
and I can still taste the gritty presence of sand
when I swallow. A memory
of my tongue running along empty shells
and a feel of sharp, unwelcome words
(I think they have left scars,
organised on my lip
like Man's meticulous placement of groynes).

An inward breath predicts seagulls hurtling to shore
and your disarming sigh brings what rocks the seas.
My emotions hurtle with force at the coast,
landing lightly, strangely. Leaking

from my eyes like spittle.

About the weather

Consistency and reason
carve cravings from me;
I find memoirs sketched in the clouds
and philosophies written by the rising sun. Golden
and ever-changing: a work in progress.
The gale never settles
for less than
destruction.
So she keeps writhing.

I feel the weather inside of me.
A rippled reflection
of what the storm hides from me.
But I am more than the thunder in my lungs makes!

It rattles, my blood weeps
and it has been raining for days now.

I hope
that you are a good swimmer.

Hurting, still

Months have sunk into years
and I think that Time
is an underqualified doctor.

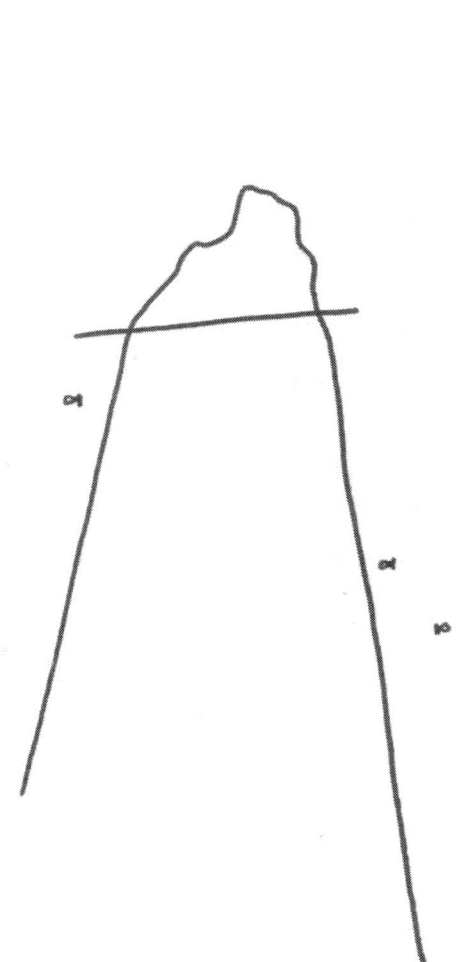

Struggling through silence

We talk until our lungs give in;
spewing sense and nonsense
until scorpions claw up our throats,
deeming our hearts too dry a climate to habit.
I guess they run from our words, too –
scuttling away from promises,
believing that we thrive best alone.
I drag my tongue across the desert of my teeth
in desperate pursuit for words, more words,
for you to lap up.

We end, both too fixated on the other
that we barely taste the panicking creatures
that we gag and choke upon.

You've lost your mind

I found your mind in lost property.
It shone out to me:
a scribble of discontent and
misery.

A note attached read:
if found, never return.

Amongst dirty jumpers,
dead phones and
broken dreams,
I left your mind
sluggishly pulsating and
bursting
at the seams.

Stronger than you think

Do not overlook me because I am small.
Because I am timid,
plentiful,
lesser.

A mere ant
in the grass.

Do not be fooled –
an ant can carry fifty times its own weight.

The strongest animal for its size.

I carry regret and
remorse and
guilt.
Yet still I march forwards,
dragging a heavy heart
behind me.

Do not be fooled –
I am
stronger than you think.

- *For Mum*

SOMEONE I'LL NEVER KNOW

Beginning / end

Hyperawareness decays
like the day does at dawn: painfully unknowingly –
until pupils are chasms that seek out the sun.

Like a drunkard passed out
in the mid-afternoon glare
– left cheek caressing
the cantankerous grass
– right cheek charred
from hours of unintentional sunbathing:
I am unknowingly passive.
Susceptible to harm way greater
than that which I am already hounding on myself.

The beginning returns only to end again. And so forth.

Lazily, I watch the sun draw
an unswerving sad face over the day
and I lie in the grass,
feeling the heavy bass of Mother Nature's heart
comfort me in Morse code.
She is retiring soon,
so her eyes turn from blue to concrete grey.
I lie flat
on her ulcered belly
and she roars.

Rubble cascades from my skin
like cremation. I am both alive and dead.
Smouldering like cancer.
Waiting.

The end comes and I expect the beginning once more.

Wokingham, Berkshire

Rain glares off the English pavestones.
It sits in my hair
and sweats down your forehead.

The night is   dark blue.

We sit by a collection of charity shops
and empty bars (it is a Monday, after all)
and we talk more about memory.

> I had my first kiss in that cinema.
> Your heart first broke on that bench.

What in Hell has happened since then?

The feeling is   unfathomable.

They've built houses
on the field that we learnt to cartwheel in.
We don't find homes in any of them.

But this town is   the world.
Households are nations
and family feuds rage with a similar force to world wars.
I have fought them,
feared them,
regretted them.

Moments lightly graze my memory
only because I have grainy slides in peeling photo albums
to prove them. Snapshots of
strangers who became loved ones
and loved ones who became

strangers.

It has been   years.
Nobody warned us how much we were going to forget.

We sip non-alcoholic wine
at the funeral of a friend
and talk about everything
apart from death. Soon it will be our turn.

The air is   cold.

Our teeth chatter
but we chat louder
as our footsteps knock on Hell's ceiling
and we walk by somewhere we used to know –

we ask questions without answers like

who says you can't play songs about death
on hospital radio?

The reply quakes
and echoes
around this demise.
I guess that quiet is a sound,
after all.

I feel   homemade:

bearing scars
where I was cut open
and sewn back together.

Faded wounds reminisce how I was scooped up
and put back together again
by the people who grew with me.

[I have since forgotten their names.]

WHO SAYS YOU CAN'T PLAY SONGS ABOUT DEATH ON HOSPITAL RADIO?

Like toothy smiles, rotting and
vanishing into past tense –

it is all

slowly

fading

away.

Grandparents

You remind me how humans are
in a way that I often forget they can be.

I grow old

We hold one another, we care.
We strike down bushes, we tear
flowers from their roots as children to make perfume.
We rip flowers from their roots as adults to apologise.

Imagine, when we are gone, petals will caress the skies!

I walk cracked streets that were once newly paved,
I amble through gardens once freshly shaved.
I grow old.

Years pass like spoiled film,
grainy, samey.
Flashes
of good and bad and good and bad
and splashes
of happy and sad and happy
and happy.

We are fighting nature for space on earth but
once we are gone
vines will greedily devour graffitied walls,
pulling on unnatural bricks and concrete until they fall.
I've seen death,
all as all,
unnatural and unfair,
not to be saved by wishes or by prayer.

Life is the burden of wear;
a price you pay for just being here.
A debt thought paid through pain and fear.

When we dissolve
fights will resolve
and be   forgotten.

Humans will evolve
and be   forgotten.
Broken homes will be strengthened
with roots so much stronger than love.
Blood will dry,
anger will dissipate,
a weight
of greed and hatred will lift,
shift from the atmosphere
and fear
will calm.

Humans make things complicated.
We
make things complicated!
Created on our need to be heard,
outdated opinions mistaken as facts –
even our frustrated facades are putting on acts!
When we are gone

the earth will be calm.

I grow old.
I watch as my muscle rots,
as my blood clots,
as my skin sags
and my bones lock.

Oh, to be young.
To watch leaves fall from oak
and grow from the earth again.
To watch seeds sprout and grow and blossom
to get cut and sprout and grow and blossom again.

When I return to dust
gentle winds shall blow lullabies
against abandoned wind chimes.

Discarded bikes will draw lifetimes
in the sand,
swallowing childhood bullies
and drowning hoodies
on street corners.

I shiver
on the bank of the river
where I grew.
Through worn eyes I picture
us
laughing in our prime
and I wonder:

where has time
gone?

We are all but the same!
Sewn like seeds, grown as grain,
one as one, regiments remain
static
in fields of themselves
that grow as tumours for miles and miles
to feed
nothing.
To rot in piles.

The years, the years;
measured in time, laughter, tears.

I count my blessings alongside my fears.

Ah, no, how my back creaks. How pain
seeps and cheats and leaps through bones
and the moans.
The moans
that leaves will rustle upon,

shaking me until my muscle is gone
with my flesh, my bones
and all that will remain are the moans.

I grow old.
Hopping
from one dull pain to another.
Stopping
at nothing.

Soon, people will harvest decay
and weeds will find a way through hospital floors
where broken hearts once mourned lost wars.

Plagued roots will map out lives
under ground where humans trod but never touched.

I work hard but I will never amount to much.
I grow old.

Green, luscious life
will fold through graveyards –
fracture tombstones –
cover faded, unknown names –
push and alter feeble remains …

Maggots will flow from rocking chair eyes,
down worry stained cheeks
into lips smeared with lies.
Flesh missing, ravaged,
rotting with flies.

And, finally,
hearts will curdle with loathing that can't forgive –
humans so anxious about image,

we forgot how to live.

Ah, no, I grow old.
I wrinkle like oak; I tarnish like gold.

Wind will blow TV static to whispers,
gales shall whither cities
and once grand sky scrapers
will only adorn
scraped knees.

I will vanish like a message in the sand.
But still the waves, they will come:

inland

       inland

              inland.

...

THANK YOU.
X

Caitlin Thornley is a 21-year-old writer from Wokingham.

She has been self publishing poetry on Instagram for just over a year and *WHO SAYS YOU CAN'T PLAY SONGS ABOUT DEATH ON HOSPITAL RADIO?* is her debut poetry collection.

Caitlin would like you all to know that her cats enjoy listening to her reading her poetry to them and suggests that you try reading this book to your pets, too.

Instagram: @caitlinthornleywords
Facebook: /caitlinthornleywords
Twitter: @caitlout

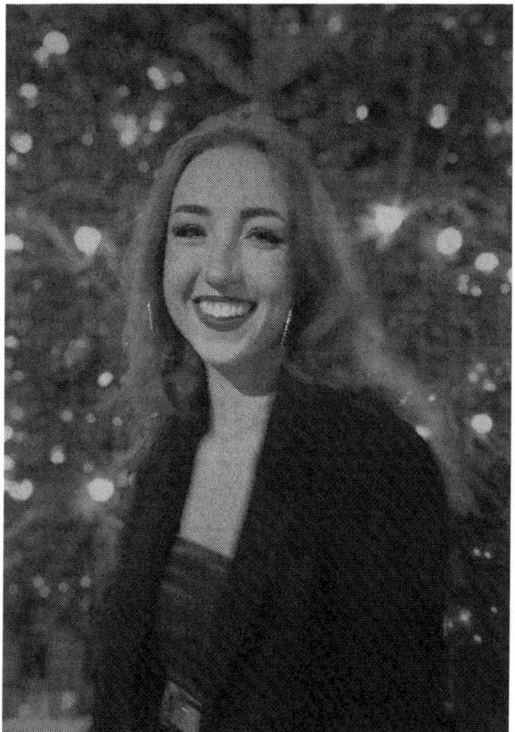

Printed in Great Britain
by Amazon